In the Name of Allah the Gracious, the Merciful

Climb the Tree of Islam. A Little Book About Big Beliefs

Copyright © 2026 by Basim Alansari

All rights reserved. No part of this publication may be reproduced, distributed, or transmitted in any form or by any means, including photocopying, recording, or other electronic or mechanical methods, without the prior written permission of the publisher, except in the case of brief quotations embodied in critical reviews and certain other noncommercial uses permitted by copyright law. For permission requests, write to the publisher, addressed "Attention: - Permissions (Climb the Tree of Islam. A Little Book About Big Beliefs)," at the email address below.

Lantern Publications
info@lanternpublications.com
www.lanternkids.com.au

A catalogue record for this book is available from the National Library of Australia

"Lantern Kids" is a subsidiary of Lantern Publications

Ordering Information:
Quantity sales. Special discounts are available on quantity purchases by corporations, associations, and others. For details, contact the distributor at the address below.

Written by: Basim Alansari
Illustrated by: Mahdi Tabatabai Yazdi

ISBN- 978-1-922583-75-8

First Edition

Please learn your lessons My kids!
To know what God permits or forbids,
Begin with the Principles of Your Faith.
Islam is to submit to what Allah saith,
Islam is built on the golden five.
Our faith, from them we derive.

The third principle, to which we adhere,
Nubuwwa or Prophethood is clear.
It's our need to have guides,
Messengers whom God the Wise decides.
Thousands of them were sent,
So that our logic, they complement.
Mohammad was their last,
To his rightful path, we hold fast

The fourth is a principle we uphold,
Despite whatever our opponents may hold,
Imamah is needed, to pass God's exams,
It is our belief in the Twelve Imams.

The fifth principle is **Ma'ad**,
When all gather in one crowd.
To be judged by God the meriful in the afterlife,
To be asked about our success and strife.

Please learn all of this by heart!
To be a thoughtful Muslim, truly smart

Salaat is to pray,
Five times in a day.
Dawn, noon, afternoon, sunset and night.
Through prayer, we gain our might.

Fasting happens during Ramadhan,
A month when evil is withdrawn.

Haj is Islam's holiest prime,
A pilgrimage once in a lifetime.

In all these matters you should follow
What scholars forbid or allow.
Choose wisely a scholar who's wise,
Who helps your Faith in God to rise!

www.ingramcontent.com/pod-product-compliance
Lightning Source LLC
Chambersburg PA
CBHW041215240426
43661CB00012B/1052